THE BARNES FOUNDATION
TWO BUILDINGS, ONE MISSION

David B. Brownlee

NEW YORK

in association with the Barnes Foundation

CONTENTS

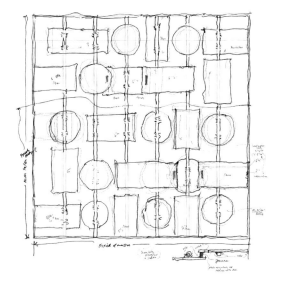

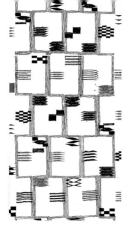

FOREWORD

The opening of the Barnes Foundation's splendid new campus on Philadelphia's Benjamin Franklin Parkway is an occasion for honoring and celebrating the extraordinary achievements of the institution's founder, Albert C. Barnes. Dr. Barnes was passionate about providing exceptional examples of art and design from across the world, the study of which would enrich all our lives. This volume is devoted to the buildings by Paul Cret and by Tod Williams and Billie Tsien, both designed to house the remarkable Barnes collection and its associated educational programs.

Some five years in the making, and a decade after the idea of moving the collection to the city was first proposed by the Barnes Board of Trustees, the realization of the new campus has been the work of many people, beginning with Dr. Bernard Watson, chair of the Barnes Foundation since 1999. At the heart of this project lies his conviction that the Barnes should and could remain a financially viable, independent educational organization, bringing Albert Barnes's vision to the people of America. Much is owed to Aileen Roberts, chair of the board's Building Committee, who has given so much time, energy, and thought to the parkway project, from the architectural search

5

onward, and to Neil Rudenstine for his keen analysis of the original building program. Deep gratitude is due also to all our other board members, our colleagues at Lincoln University, and our donors, who have believed the Foundation's mission to enlighten is as relevant to the twenty-first century as it was ninety years ago. I extend special thanks, of course, to our architects, Tod Williams and Billie Tsien, and to Philip Ryan.

David Brownlee, Shapiro-Weitzenhoffer Professor at the University of Pennsylvania, has marvelously captured the journey taken by our architects and consultants in conceiving and then executing the translation of the Barnes experience from Merion to Philadelphia. His immense knowledge of Philadelphia's architectural history is lightly worn and gracefully delivered. The Foundation is deeply grateful to him for undertaking this project and creating such a highly readable and lively record. At the Barnes Foundation, my thanks go to Chief Curator Judith F. Dolkart and Director of Publications Johanna Halford-MacLeod, both of whom have worked closely with the author and the publisher to bring the volume to completion; to Project Executive William McDowell and his assistant Beth Lillis, who have been so supportive of Professor Brownlee's research into the design process for the parkway facility; to Archivist and Librarian Katy Rawdon and archivists Barbara Beaucar and Allison Jai O'Dell who assisted with the history of Paul Cret's designs for Merion; and to Deborah Lenert, visual resources manager, who gathered the images for this book.

Derek Gillman
Executive Director and President
The Barnes Foundation

OPPOSITE: FLOOR MOSAIC, INSPIRED BY THE LIAR'S CLOTH PATTERN OF KENTE TEXTILES, AT THE ENTRANCE TO THE LIGHT COURT, PHILADELPHIA. MADE BY NELSON LONDONO, ARTSAICS.

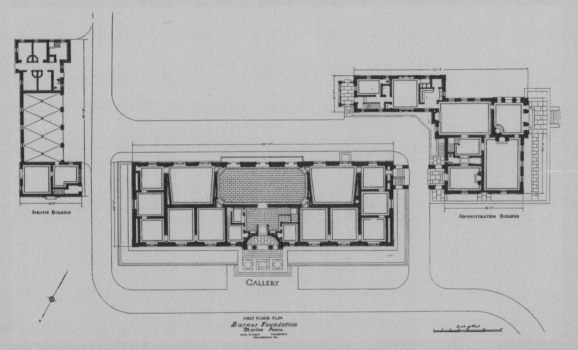

SERVICE BUILDING

ADMINISTRATION BUILDING

GALLERY

FIRST FLOOR PLAN
Barnes Foundation
Merion Penna
PAUL P. CRET   ARCHITECT
PHILADELPHIA, PA.

Scale of Feet

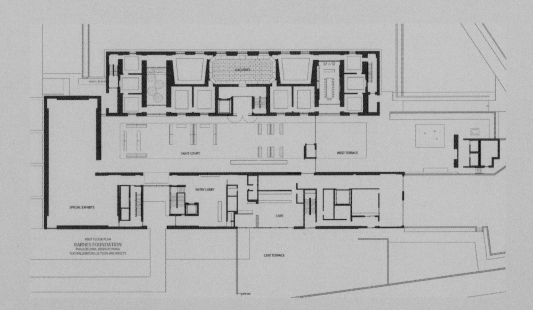

GALLERIES

LIGHT COURT

WEST TERRACE

ENTRY LOBBY

SPECIAL EXHIBITS

CAFE

FIRST FLOOR PLAN
BARNES FOUNDATION
PHILADELPHIA, PENNSYLVANIA
TOD WILLIAMS BILLIE TSIEN ARCHITECTS

CAFE TERRACE

ONE VOICE

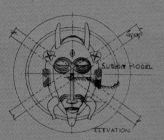

The two buildings of the Barnes Foundation are kindred spirits. Built between 1922 and 1925 on Latch's Lane in Merion, Pennsylvania, and between 2007 and 2012 on the Benjamin Franklin Parkway in Philadelphia, they are separated by four and a half miles, nine decades, and a fiery controversy about moving a great art collection, but they speak with one voice about their institution's mission of art education. This is not simply because the Foundation agreed, as a condition of the court's approval in 2004 of the move to the parkway, that the new building would replicate the layout of the galleries and the elaborate scheme of picture

hanging from Merion. Beyond that, Tod Williams and Billie Tsien, the architects of the new Barnes, devoted themselves to creating a sequence of outdoor and indoor spaces that, like Paul Cret's design at Merion, carries visitors away from the quotidian and guides them to encounter great art in a contemplative but concentrated manner.

A historical coincidence buttresses this bridge of architectural intentions. The new Barnes is located next to another building by Cret, the Rodin Museum (1926–1929), built just after the galleries in Merion. And the formal gardens that frame the Rodin Museum were devised by Jacques Gréber,

OPPOSITE: JACQUES
GRÉBER. PROPOSED
GARDEN ON THE
BENJAMIN FRANKLIN
PARKWAY AT
TWENTIETH STREET, 1919

FOLLOWING SPREAD:
NORTH ELEVATION
OF GALLERY AND
ADMINISTRATION
BUILDING, NOVEMBER
18 AND 28, 1922

who, earlier in his career, had sketched similar small gardens for the full length of the parkway, including a proposal for the site now occupied by the Barnes. The structure of the new garden by landscape architect Laurie Olin is unselfconsciously sympathetic to Gréber's forgotten design, perhaps because Olin's firm was engaged, while working on the Barnes, in restoring Gréber's landscape at the Rodin Museum. In terms of architecture and landscape design, the arrival of the Barnes Foundation on the Benjamin Franklin Parkway is thus a kind of homecoming.

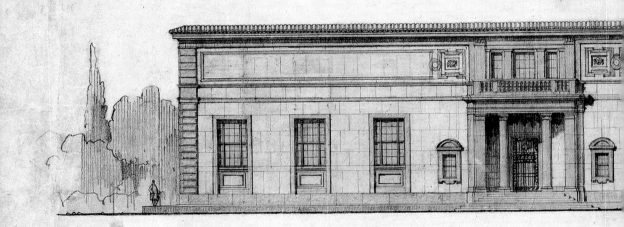

FRONT ELEVATION OF PICTURE GALLE

THE · BARNES · FOUNDATION

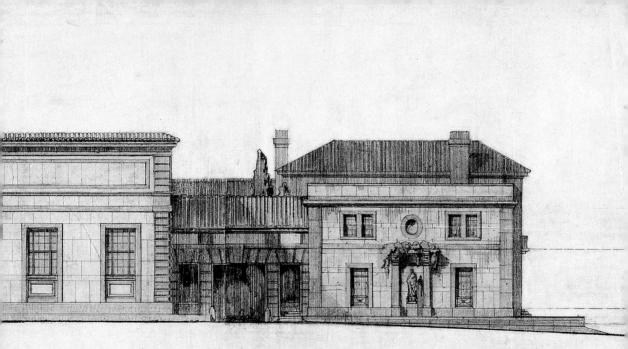

ON·PA

· NORTH · WEST · ELEVATION ·

MERION

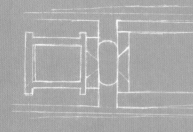

Albert C. Barnes (1872–1951), the chemist, pharmaceutical entrepreneur, and art collector, was a decisive man. His character is imprinted on the art institution that he swiftly created in 1922, founded on the pragmatic philosophy of his mentor John Dewey, devoted to the ideal of democratic education that he had pioneered with the workers in his factory, and filled with exemplary modern art, the principal objects of study. To design a building for this enterprise he selected Paul Philippe Cret (1876–1945), who had come to Philadelphia from his native France in 1903 to lead the architecture program at the University of Pennsylvania.

By the 1920s Cret had established Penn as the foremost architecture school in the U.S. and secured his own reputation as a leading American practitioner of the kind of rational, modernized classicism that he had learned at the École des Beaux-Arts in Paris, and which he now taught in Philadelphia.

Barnes's quickly accumulating wealth came from the sale of Argyrol, the effective antiseptic silver compound that he had invented. He had begun to collect art seriously in 1912, and he first

ALBERT C. BARNES IN 1923   PAUL CRET IN 1925

hung his burgeoning collection in the big stone Gothic house Lauraston, named after his wife, that he built on Latch's Lane in Merion in 1905. Barnes took great interest in the neighboring real estate. In 1912 and 1913 he bought and developed several large properties at the east end of Latch's Lane, and soon he was angling to buy Red Slates, the Victorian house in which Joseph Lapsley Wilson had lived since 1880. Barnes was especially interested in the impressive arboretum, with a very large collection of rare specimen trees that Wilson had acquired and nurtured.

In October 1922, Barnes brought the several parts of his project together with great velocity. While his lawyer worked on the establishment of a Barnes Foundation, he engaged Cret to design a teaching gallery for the new institution, sketching out his architectural needs in a memo on October 12.[1] The next day he finalized the acquisition of Red Slates and its arboretum as a site. Within a week

Cret had produced a sketch design and discussed it several times with his client, who was pleased and praised him as America's "best architect" to his favorite Parisian dealer, Paul Guillaume, on October 20. By November samples of imported French limestone were being inspected, and Cret was preparing a detailed set of "preliminary study" drawings (see pages 16-17). On November 29 the architect

LAWRENCE VISSCHER BOYD. LAURASTON, MERION, COMPLETED 1905

completed a short essay explaining the shared principles on which he and Barnes had based the design, and on December 4 the Commonwealth of Pennsylvania chartered the new foundation. When Barnes sailed for France on December 12, his foundation was a fact and the design of the building that he had described to his architect just two months earlier was complete.

This rapid work was possible because Barnes embraced Cret's thinking about art museums, which the architect had already demonstrated in his design for the Detroit Institute of Arts, where ground had just been broken. Deviating from the preference for skylighted exhibition galleries that had prevailed in museum design since the nineteenth century, Cret believed that museum rooms should be lit from the side by conventional windows. In the planning report that he wrote in 1920 for Detroit, he had also commended varied smaller rooms, whose domestic scale was less

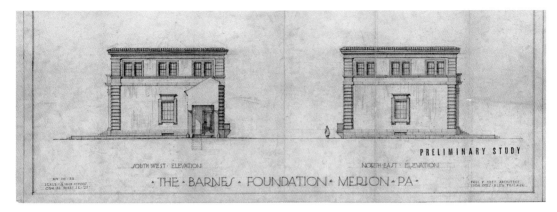

END ELEVATIONS OF THE GALLERY, NOVEMBER 20, 1928

likely to exhaust viewers, and his early sketch plans for that museum showed a garden courtyard directly beyond the entrance hall, ensuring that visitors were refreshed and inspired by a glimpse of nature before they looked at art.[2] Barnes, who displayed his collection in his own house and who aspired to locate his foundation in an arboretum, surely found Cret's thinking congenial.

In January 1923 the newspapers announced the chartering of the new foundation and published the design of the new gallery, shown flanked by an administration building (which would also serve as the Barnes home) and a service building containing an automobile garage and stables (see page 8). The essay that Cret had written in November now

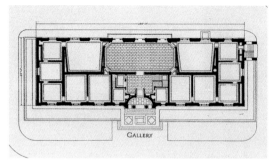

FIRST-FLOOR PLAN OF THE GALLERY, AS PUBLISHED IN 1926

appeared in *The Arts* magazine, proudly claiming that the building would be "architecturally of an entirely new type."[3] Expanding on what he had said about his Detroit design, but apparently speaking for both himself and his client, he explained that the galleries aimed to re-create "those conditions that the painter would wish for the display of his work," based on the debatable premise that artists would wish others to see their work lit from the side, as it had been in their studios. More convincingly, Cret also argued that skylighted galleries imprisoned the average museum visitor, who, "jailed between the walls, longs very soon for a glimpse of the outdoors."

To improve further the experience of viewers, the rooms would be of moderate size and varied in dimension and shape. Two of the rooms on each floor were trapezoidal in plan, apparently due to the theory that the angled walls would better catch light from the window. Cret explained that there was "no useless corridor, but a simple circulation through the rooms dividing each floor in two circuits, starting from and leading to the central hall." That central, two-story space, with "huge windows and a balcony overlooking the garden," was intended for the display of art as well as music performances and lectures. It was this purposeful space, rather than a system of stairs and corridors, that tied the building together with a compositional rigor like that with which Barnes hung the paintings on his walls. And the compact floor plan, pulled into a slender rectangle, was also economical to build, which the business-minded chemist surely appreciated. The striking simplicity and clarity of this concept, which would define the character of the Barnes Foundation

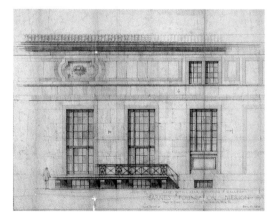

PARTIAL SOUTH ELEVATION OF THE GALLERY, DECEMBER 8, 1922

even after it moved to Philadelphia ninety years later, derived from the special congruence in the thinking of two strong-willed men.

The vocabulary of forms that Cret adopted for the exterior was a simplified, twentieth-century version of the Italian Renaissance, and it was built of imported French limestone in two contrasting shades; rosy Pouillenay was used for the trim, while the walling was built of creamy Coutarnoux. This introduced far more color than was typical for American monumental architecture of the time, which was usually built of pallid gray-white Indiana limestone, and Barnes was immensely pleased by the effect. He likened it to the colors in Cézanne.[4]

Even more modernist was Barnes's plan for the building's sculptural ornament. While in Paris in December 1922, he contacted the sculptor Jacques Lipchitz (1891–1973) and commissioned five bas-reliefs and a freestanding sculpture for the exterior of the new foundation. Lipchitz's late-cubist panels

THE
BARNES FOUNDATION
MCMXXIII

replaced the conventional carving of flower baskets that Cret had shown on his drawings. Indeed, the plain geometries of Cret's simplified classical architecture were very hospitable toward Lipchitz's angular depictions of musicians, musical instruments, and fruit, and the two French artists collaborated cordially. Barnes subsequently acquired two additional reliefs from Lipchitz, for which Cret found places on the buildings. The collector crowed to Paul Guillaume on January 15, 1923, "When the public see those Lipchitz carvings right on the front of the building, they will say I am not only a radical but a Bolshevist."

Barnes also strove to mark the building with his other great artistic passion, African art, which he had been learning about from Guillaume and buying from his Paris gallery. This was most strikingly visible in the decoration of the entrance apse

OPPOSITE: PAUL CRET. DESIGN FOR ENTRANCE TILE WORK, FEBRUARY 1923

JACQUES LIPCHITZ. *RECLINING FIGURE WITH GUITAR*, 1923, SOUTH FACADE

framing the front door, which Cret had turned over to his friend J. H. Dulles (Joe) Allen. Allen's Enfield Pottery and Tile Works, located outside Philadelphia in Montgomery County, had supplied Arts and Crafts–style decoration for several of the architect's earlier projects.

Cret's first drawing for tile work was robust but classically inflected, but, apparently prompted by Barnes, he soon decided to insert African motifs,

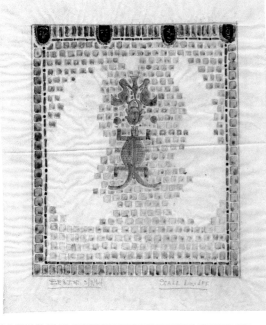

J. H. DULLES ALLEN. DESIGN FOR ENTRANCE TILE WORK, MARCH 8, 1924

asking the collector for materials on "negro art" on March 1, 1923. This inspired a series of vibrant further studies, which he reviewed with Barnes and turned over to Allen for development and execution in July. The upper register of the decoration featured ceramic replicas of statues from Mali, Gabon, Côte d'Ivoire, and Congo standing caryatid-like beneath the ceiling. These were based on photographs that Barnes supplied to the designer. Allen subsequently recommended tiling the large panels on either side of the door, originally shown as plaster, and centering in each field a striking crocodile motif taken from a Baule door from Côte d'Ivoire in his client's collection. Barnes, whose collecting would soon expand to embrace American decorative arts, was delighted by Allen's contemporary craftsmanship, joyfully predicting that the tile-lined exedra would be "a corker" in a note to the designer on May 20, 1924.

African motifs also appeared in the building's decorative iron- and plasterwork. The railings of the balconies bore African masks, and masks were also quietly worked into the cornice of the principal, double-height gallery. These details were designed by Roy Larson, a gifted young architect who had just graduated from Cret's program at Penn and gone to work for his professor (see page 10).

Even while these design components were being worked out, Albert Barnes pressed to erect the building as soon as possible. Stone was ordered from France—and its price shrewdly negotiated—in 1922, before the construction specifications were complete. At the same time, he sought to launch his educational and exhibition programs in advance of having a home for them. He contacted local universities about hosting the instructional activities of the foundation, and he briefly exhibited—to some acclaim—his latest acquisitions of modern painting and African sculpture in Guillaume's Paris gallery between January 22 and February 3, 1923.

Despite these successes and the generally warm reception of Barnes's project in the American press when it was announced in January, he was soon reminded of the difficulties to be surmounted in winning broader acceptance for his views about modern art. This was made plain when, buoyed by the reports he heard about the exhibition of his art in Paris, he arranged to exhibit another sampling of his paintings and sculpture at the Pennsylvania Academy of the Fine Arts from April 11 until May 9. This was accompanied by a catalog in which he explained the new art. The reviews this time, devoted to modern art and not Barnes's new institution, were alternately uncomprehending and excoriating, and the artists were variously condemned as madmen, degenerates, and charlatans.[5]

Barnes was already known to be cantankerous, and although he was not identified by name or

criticized in the reviews, he lashed out at the critics of the exhibition with special fury and personal animus. In the wake of this episode, the actual construction of the new building, whose design had been so swiftly and agreeably planned, was marked by acrimony. Barnes interested himself (or meddled) in every aspect of the project and, because he lived next door to the site, stopped by regularly to check on progress. The new mood was signaled on April 12, one day after the show opened at the Pennsylvania Academy, when he wrote in an offensive tone to Cret about the inadequate measures taken to safeguard the good topsoil on the building site in preparation for construction. Cret drafted a long reply and sent a short one.[6]

Barnes and Cret shared the goal of getting the building roofed before the onset of severe weather in December. This was put at risk when stonecutters

began a three-month strike on June 2, but Barnes was convinced that Cret's faulty supervision of the project was to blame for a good deal of the slow progress. On September 5 he launched an epistolary fusillade against his architect, who had just returned from his usual summer visit to France. Barnes, in his characteristic bullying mode, sent a series of messages over the next four days in which he complained about the "somnolence, negligence, [and] spinelessness" (September 5) and "boneheaded superintendence" (September 9) of Cret's office and observed sarcastically that "with a dead man functioning as superintendent it is no wonder that the operation has long since degenerated into a badly conducted funeral" (September 7).

Cret, his suggestion that they meet to discuss the problem rebuffed, replied gracefully on September 10 that "the situation is not as black as you paint it." Counseling that delays were unavoidable in construction work and that they were building for history, he offered his French-speaking client a proverb: *Le Temps ne respecte pas ce que l'on fait sans lui* (Time does not respect what is done without taking time). Barnes's tone quieted a little, but he continued to rant about the inability of John Hagan, the stone contractor, to mobilize sufficient men and equipment. Cret again replied with a little parable, handwritten in French, on September 28: "There are a number of differences between the Egyptian monks of the fourth century and modern workers. They had, for example, the bad habit of working long hours without pay, and also of ignoring that recent victory of the proletariat, the strike. It is very regrettable that we have not been able to hire a team of them to work at Merion." Cret was no fool. He kept a typed and dated copy of this note in his files.[7]

Barnes enlarged the scope of his correspondence with his architect on October 23, complaining facetiously, but with underlying seriousness,

about the newspapers' characterization of his foundation as a "public" museum. Stressing that "admission will only be by card issued to those people whom the Board of Directors consider are fit subjects to be benefited by the educational assets of the Foundation," and obviously smarting from

JACQUES LIPCHITZ. *MUSICAL INSTRUMENTS WITH BASKET OF FRUIT AND GRAPES*, 1923, NORTH FACADE OF GALLERY, WITH ROUNDEL TO RIGHT

the hostile reception accorded to his paintings by "the prominentists [*sic*] that one meets in the art circles of Philadelphia," he asked Cret to design "some mechanical device … to give point to our intentions concerning eunuchs, morons, boobs, professional exploiters, and general counterfeits." As examples of the undeserving frauds, he named two Philadelphia art critics, the City Parks Association secretary, the president of the Pennsylvania Academy of the Fine Arts, and the president of the Art Alliance, concluding, "I thought of a mitrailleuse [machine gun], an electric chair, a loose stone leading to an underground dungeon, but all those devices are too subtle."

Despite the summer strike, the building was built up to the roof before winter, and by early January 1924, Lipchitz's panels were mounted on the upper walls. This set off what was, for once, a substantive dispute between Barnes and Cret. The collector had apparently not noticed on Cret's

drawings that the cubist panels were to be set into a subtle pattern of masonry framing that wrapped around the upper story of the building, including a roundel adjacent to each of the bas-reliefs on the entrance facade. Seeing the sculpture in place, Barnes lashed out on January 25: "To put a circle, a mere and disbalanced gesture, alongside a creation of a great artist is certainly not in keeping with any principle of art or life that will stand analysis." He was further incensed by the report that some of Cret's assistants had disparaged Lipchitz's work. Cret once again drafted a long reply and sent a short one, offering to simplify the stonework if it was "absolutely necessary" but pointing out that Lipchitz had worked for a year from drawings that clearly showed the criticized pattern.

Over the next ten weeks Cret prepared six simpler patterns (see page 18) while Barnes did his utmost to demoralize his architect. On a single day, February 25, he sent four letters that attacked Cret from all directions—questioning his competence as a supervisor of the contractors and stone suppliers, undermining his supervisory relationship with Joe Allen, and threatening to ask Lipchitz what he thought of the roundels and tell him of the slighting comments overheard from Cret's assistants. Cret prepared several furious replies the next day, complaining that Barnes treated him "as you would not treat your chauffeur" and offering to resign.[8] These were not sent, however, because, as the lawyer whom Cret consulted later reminded him, "Dr. Barnes followed up the letter which caused you so much concern by a personal visit … which resulted in Dr. Barnes assuring you of his appreciation and co-operation and withdrawing any remarks reflecting upon your work."[9] While Barnes prepared a draft of the critical letter that he threatened to send to Lipchitz on March 12, he revised this and simply asked for the sculptor's opinion of the installed bas-reliefs as shown in photographs. Lipchitz replied on March 29 that he was "content," and Barnes decided to leave the circles as they were.

Cret had learned to handle Barnes, who now deputed his wife to oversee the remaining interior work, which stretched through the summer and into the fall. Although the mood was tranquil compared to the earlier phases of the project, there were needlessly ferocious complaints about the linoleum floor in the kitchen, the lighting fixtures in the dining room, and the picture rail in the painting galleries. For absurdity, none of these exchanges matched what Barnes called "the matter of the linen-closet."[10] Although the shelving in the closet had been built in accordance with the construction documents, it did not please Laura Barnes, and she and her husband were incensed by the estimate that rebuilding it would cost an extra $100. "This is the limit in switching on to others the responsibility for the habitual negligence

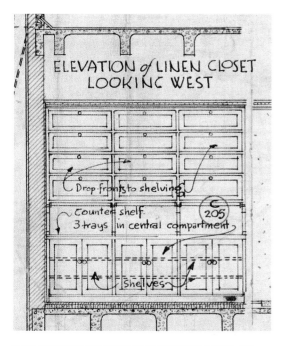

ELEVATION of LINEN CLOSET LOOKING WEST

Drop fronts to shelving

Counter shelf.
3 trays in central compartment

C
205

Shelves

LINEN CLOSET SHELVING, DETAIL OF CONSTRUCTION DRAWING, 1923

and mistakes which have, from the start, resulted from the disorder of your organization," Dr. Barnes wrote on October 23. Cret again consulted his lawyer, who wisely suggested doing nothing, although for a while "Gentlemen" replaced the personal salutation in Cret's letters to his client.

By February 1925 the building was complete, at a cost of nearly $550,000, and Barnes was working furiously to hang his paintings.[11] On February 16, perhaps unexpectedly, he wrote to Cret to suggest that he host a "Paul Cret Day" for his friends in the new building, although he forbade him from inviting "social maggots," a few of whom he named. This happy event was held on the afternoon of Sunday, March 8, followed shortly by the formal opening, with a speech by John Dewey, on March 19.

In 1925 and as now, visitors to the Barnes made their way up the curved entrance driveway to the quiet, warm-colored building, which greeted them beneath the entrance portico with the varied textures

and bold African motifs of Joe Allen's Enfield tile work. Inside, the modest entrance hall opened directly into the main, two-story gallery, whose tall windows, looking out onto the arboretum, could be seen from the front door. In the lunettes above those three windows Henri Matisse would hang his specially commissioned mural *The Dance* in 1933.

Leaving the Main Gallery from either end, visitors passed through a circuit of smaller galleries, each carefully hung with the symmetrical "ensembles" of paintings that Barnes designed to inspire thoughtful analysis. He rearranged these ensembles throughout his life, adding new acquisitions and incorporating his widening range of interests—notably metalwork, American decorative arts, and Native American art. The architectural experience was small in scale but enormous in its aesthetic intensity, as the visitor moved directly from one dense and rich artistic encounter to the next. Explaining this in 1926, Cret wrote that

ABOVE: FROM THE FOYER INTO THE MAIN GALLERY
OPPOSITE: MAIN ENTRANCE TO THE GALLERY

the Barnes Foundation showed that "a building of limited size, with a simple plan, comprising rooms with a sort of intimacy, may escape from that character that has earned for art galleries the definition of 'cemeteries of works of art.'"[12]

While Cret described the "general aspect" of the exterior as Italian Renaissance, his simplified classical detailing was by turns mannerist and modern. He also subverted the formality of the design wherever decorum allowed. Although the administration building showed a grave, symmetrical, and parapeted facade to the front, in the rear it revealed an asymmetrical composition of three units of different scale, two of which were capped by red tile roofs. In the diminutive courtyard between the gallery and the administration building, this picturesque sensibility held sway, as five distinct architectural masses came together and Cret composed a facade with four windows of

LEFT: MAIN GALLERY
PREVIOUS SPREAD: GALLERY 10

ADMINISTRATION BUILDING AND BARNES RESIDENCE, 1945

ABOVE: GALLERY WINDOW. OPPOSITE: SERVICE COURTYARD

different sizes and shapes and a diagonal chimney mass. The same sophisticated informality could be seen in the service building.

In adopting this vocabulary, Paul Cret showed respect for the gentle naturalism that prevailed throughout the arboretum, and also for Albert Barnes's taste for "picturesque and quaint" French village architecture, about which he wrote to Guillaume on August 15, 1922, on the eve of establishing his foundation. But this was not a nostalgic reference. In the tile roofs and ocher masonry there was more than a whisper of the rural buildings that Paul Cézanne had depicted in paintings that Barnes owned. Like the French painter and the American chemist who collected his work, Cret saw the basis for a potent modern art in the patterns of the vernacular, and such shared artistic values allowed Cret and Barnes to create a successful building despite the petty disputes that attended its making.

THE PARKWAY

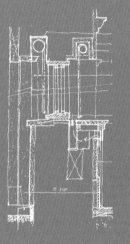

Like the galleries in Merion, the new home of the Barnes Foundation on the Benjamin Franklin Parkway, inaugurated in 2012, is a vital work of modern architecture shaped by Albert Barnes's educational mission. It, too, was created against a backdrop of controversy—the dispute over the relocation of the collection from Merion to Philadelphia, which had little bearing on the architecture.

Designed by the architectural team of Tod Williams (1943–) and Billie Tsien (1949–), the new building is the outcome of a project begun a decade earlier, when the financially pressed institution, with the promise of funding from major foundations, began to plan for the move. That change required court permission, and on December 13, 2004, Judge Stanley Ott of the Montgomery County Orphans' Court accepted the Barnes Foundation's argument that its financial situation was untenable and approved its petition to re-create its galleries in central Philadelphia.

After Judge Ott's ruling, the project swiftly took on an architectural dimension, which was made possible by major grants and promises of funding, conditional on the move of the collection, from the Pew Charitable Trusts, the Lenfest and Annenberg foundations, the Commonwealth of Pennsylvania, and other major foundations and donors, and by the important offer by Philadelphia mayor John Street of a prominent site near the city's other cultural institutions. An enlarged board of trustees was also permitted by Judge Ott's ruling, and among the new trustees appointed in January 2005 was the leader of the nascent building campaign, Aileen Roberts. Roberts, who had a strong background in landscape architecture and was one of

TOD WILLIAMS AND BILLIE TSIEN

Philadelphia's most generous supporters of cultural institutions, would chair the large Building Committee.

The committee aimed high. They hired James Polshek, an eminent architect of museums and

educational buildings and former dean of architecture at Columbia University, to prepare an analysis of the program and site. Polshek's team conducted extensive interviews with trustees, staff, and other Barnes stakeholders in the summer and fall of 2006 and worked with the Barnes's recently hired director, Derek Gillman, a scholar of Chinese art with a long, continent-spanning dossier of museum leadership and building projects. Gillman collaborated closely with another new board member, Harvard's former president Neil Rudenstine, who chaired the Program Committee, to establish the requirements for the new building.

The Polshek report, issued on January 2, 2007, catalogued the new classrooms, auditorium, staff offices, conservation labs, library, art-handling facilities, and restaurant that could now be provided. The total was 119,205 square feet—four times larger than the building in Merion.[13] It also provided a detailed analysis of the prominent site that had been assigned on the Benjamin Franklin Parkway, Philadelphia's great, City Beautiful–era civic boulevard. The highly visible location, between Paul Cret's Rodin Museum and Logan Square, had previously been occupied rather incongruously by a detention center for juvenile offenders.

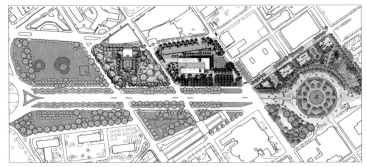

LAURIE OLIN. LANDSCAPE PLAN SHOWING THE SITE OF THE BARNES FOUNDATION ON THE BENJAMIN FRANKLIN PARKWAY, BETWEEN THE RODIN MUSEUM AND LOGAN SQUARE, JUNE 2009

More consequentially, the report eloquently captured the spirit of the Barnes Foundation, describing it as an institution of education rather than simply a place to display art, whose galleries would be "primary teaching spaces." The document echoed the commitment made by the Barnes trustees in their petition to the Orphans' Court in September 2002 to "install the artworks in the new location in accordance with Dr. Barnes's principles."[14] It specified that the Foundation planned to replicate the installation in Center City, maintaining not only the relationships of the objects within each ensemble but also those from wall to wall; each new gallery room should therefore take the shape, size, and proportions of the original spaces. It also noted that special attention would be paid to improving the gallery lighting from both natural and artificial sources.

More generally, but no less tellingly, the program analysis highlighted the "implicit pairing of art and landscape" in the arboretum in Merion and called for

this to be maintained on the parkway. It specified, too, a design that encouraged "contemplation and study." Architects were directed to "effectively and sensitively modulate the character and scale of the building from the more lively and dynamic spaces to the quieter and more contemplative."

The thoughtful specificity of the program shaped all that followed. Also of enormous importance was the foundation's very high architectural ambition. In the same spirit in which Albert Barnes had hired America's "best architect" in 1922, Roberts and Gillman designed an extraordinary architect selection process. To guide it, they employed Martha Thorne, the city planner and architectural curator who since 2005 had served as the executive director of the international Pritzker Prize, the annual award that is often referred to as architecture's Nobel Prize. Thorne convened the Building Committee on February 5, 2007, sketched out a two-tier selection process, and proclaimed that her goal was to choose the architect "with the lowest possible risk … of producing only 'a very good building.'" The committee was further advised by Dean Gary Hack of the University of Pennsylvania and Suzanne Stephens of *Architectural Record*.

Requests for qualifications went out to more than thirty architects on February 28, accompanied by the Polshek program study and reiterating its main themes. Twenty-two replies were received by April 3, six of them from Pritzker Prize winners (and a seventh, subsequent winner). The committee worked quickly, and six finalists were publicly announced on April 27.

Tod Williams and Billie Tsien had completed several highly regarded educational buildings and two museums at the time they received the invitation from the Barnes. The selectors were impressed by their Skirkanich Hall (2003–2006) at the University of Pennsylvania and by the American Folk Art Museum (2000–2002). Both are narrow buildings, one squeezed between two historic buildings (at Penn) and the other inserted into a narrow site next to the Museum of Modern Art in New York. They embody many of their architects' principles of locating and making architecture and inhabiting it with human activity. Each is intimately associated with the ground on which it stands, and each is faced with materials that seem unusually substantial—mottled glazed tiles in Philadelphia and enormous roughly cast bronze panels in New York. Their textures are reminders of the craftsmanship that made them. Inside, circulation is wed with the two demanding programs, filling the tall, skinny museum's generous stairs with art and the engineering lab's multilevel passages with the hubbub of students. In both, the confinement of a narrow site is compensated for by generous vertical spaces that rise through the buildings, filling them with light and air.

Williams and Tsien were delighted by the invitation, and, "ashamed" that they (like many art lovers) had never seen the idiosyncratic museum in Merion, they quickly

RENDERING OF THE BARNES FOUNDATION, PERSPECTIVE FROM THE WEST, SHOWING THE MONITOR OVER THE LIGHT COURT, OCTOBER 2009

arranged a visit.[15] Williams later recalled the "epiphany" that they experienced as they turned off Latch's Lane and proceeded up the curving drive toward the gallery. "The first impression was … of entering a garden," Tsien said, and they resolved that they must re-create such "a place in a garden." Inside, by contrast, they were "overwhelmed by the density of the art," and the telling juxtaposition of the disparate forms of natural and human creativity came to define the Barnes for them.

Like the other invited participants, Williams and Tsien were led to these impressions by the Polshek report. They quickly refined those generalities in the crucible of their artistic imaginations, and their response, sent under a cover letter dated April 2, 2007, seemed fresh and focused. "We believe that one of the most critical tasks of any design for the new facility will be establishing a precinct of quiet and tranquility," they wrote. "To achieve that effect elements of the program

GARDEN, LOOKING TOWARD ENTRANCE, OCTOBER 2009

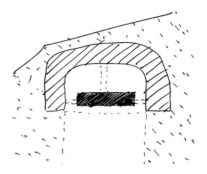

CONCEPTUAL SKETCH PLAN, APRIL 2007

might be arranged around the Merion galleries as a wrapper."[16] Illustrating this idea was a tiny sketch plan showing the distinctive bar-shaped Merion building standing in the mouth of a protective U-shaped support structure that contained the additional space that was prescribed. The sketch was accompanied by a photograph of a Zen garden in Japan.

The other five architects selected to interview for the job were an international who's who: Tadao Ando, the firm of Diller Scofidio + Renfro, Kengo Kuma, Thom Mayne, and Rafael Moneo. Given the strong guidance of the program document, it is unsurprising that they presented their ideas with similar rhetoric, but the forms of their submissions were surprisingly varied. Perhaps most distinctive were the proposals of Moneo and Diller Scofidio + Renfro. Moneo converted each of the rooms from Merion into a freestanding unit, sheltered under a vast roof umbrella and open on all sides to the landscape. Elizabeth Diller explained that her firm aimed to create an "urban refuge" for the collection by placing the bar of the Merion galleries atop an artificial landscape that would set off and shelter it while accommodating the new facilities underneath. They offered three alternative arrangements.

Neither disassembling the Cret building nor setting it atop a sea of tilted lawn, Williams and Tsien took a less flamboyant route. Recalling their epiphany that the original building was "a place in the garden" but acknowledging the challenges to that formulation

on an urban site, they prepared a PowerPoint presentation for their interview on August 10 in which they explained, "Rather than reproducing the current Merion site diagram (i.e., surrounding the new building with a garden), our initial strategy centers on identifying 'fault lines' within the original gallery layout which can be exploited to bring the gardens into the building proper." A little diagram contrasted "a gallery in a garden" (as at Merion) with a "garden in a gallery" (which they proposed). Their analysis had

BILLIE TSIEN. CONCEPT SKETCH, JULY 2007

showed that they could drop two greenery-filled light courts into the bar of the gallery building, retaining all the room sizes and their relative positions but introducing light and a welcome respite from the relentless succession of overfilled galleries. With disarming wit they diagrammed this as a sliced Philadelphia hoagie.

An elegant wood-and-plastic model, made in the last week before the interview, presented these ideas in a more conventionally architectural form, with the intended leafy courts shown as vertical inserts of green Plexiglas. Also visible was the designers' intention to insert a full mezzanine of educational spaces between the two floors of galleries—a proposition that was abandoned as they developed a better understanding of the section of the original building and the budget for the new one. As in the little diagram from early April, the large amount of new support space was provided in a low ring of buildings to the north of the gallery; these were to be connected to the galleries underground, the whole pulled

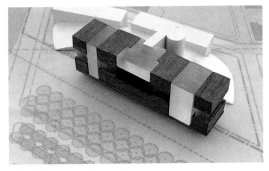

MODEL FOR INTERVIEW, JULY 2007

together by an enormous, round elevator-classroom that would transport students between the gallery and educational levels.

There was a happy sympathy between the architects and the Building Committee, who followed up with a visit to Williams and Tsien in their office on Central Park South on August 24. About an hour after departing, the committee called back to say that the job was theirs.

On the basis of a smaller, 90,000-square-foot program, which Rudenstine and Gillman created to bring the project within reach of its budget, Williams and Tsien began to work in late fall on four alternative "concept designs," each based on a different notion of how the "treasure box of galleries" from Merion could be connected to new facilities. These were explained to the board at a special retreat at the Comcast Center in Philadelphia on January 19, 2008.[17] From this thoughtful starting point, Williams and Tsien developed the design over the next eight months. While this entailed more twists and turns and took longer than Cret's work with Barnes, it was quite unlike the deliberative process that Williams and Tsien preferred and had explained in a memorable essay called "Slowness."[18]

Keeping this complex, fast-moving project on track required expertise, and at the end of January the foundation hired William McDowell, an experienced architect and skilled construction manager, to serve

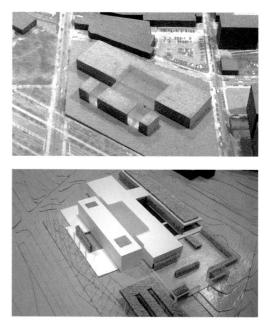

TOP: MODEL OF "MEDALLION" CONCEPT, JANUARY 2008
ABOVE: MODEL OF "THREE BARS IN A GARDEN," FEBRUARY 2008

as the building project executive. McDowell had managed development for Philadelphia's Brickstone Realty, Amtrak, and the Philadelphia Redevelopment Authority, and he would work with the architects on an almost daily basis.

One of the January concept designs, dubbed the "campus," was a development of the little hoagie model, with the Merion gallery sitting in front of a low crescent of support buildings with a studied informality that echoed the architects' other institutional work, like the much-praised Neurosciences Institute at La Jolla (1993–1995). (That building had been admired by the committee when they visited it after deciding that Williams and Tsien would be finalists.) However, this mode of organization was rejected along with the so-called "block" and "ground plane" concepts in favor of a more formal concept design that they called the "medallion." In this, the gallery wing was the "medallion," hung from a rectangular C-shaped necklace of ancillary services, with a

multistory atrium held between them. This formality was in keeping with both the monumental classical architecture of the parkway and Cret's original building, and it also reflected the somewhat quieter spirit of the architects' recent work; Williams said that his mantra at the time was "calmer is better."

By the March 1 meeting of the Building Committee, the medallion design had been developed, with a

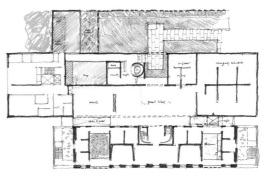

TOD WILLIAMS. SKETCH PLAN, APRIL 4, 2008

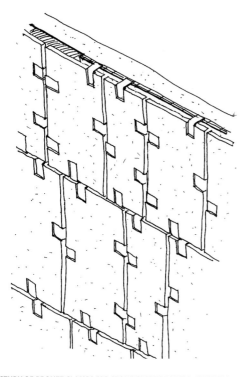

STUDY OF BRONZE CLAMPS FOR STONE FACADE PANELS, MAY 2008

green-roofed parking garage added at the north to create "three bars in a garden"—the gallery building, new support-services block, and parking facility. The main features of the vitally important garden were also presented: an entrance grove at the southeast corner and a route marked by water features and framed by hedges and allées of trees that led the visitor to enter from the north through the necklace, rather than directly from the parkway into the gallery block. While this upset conventional thinking, it disengaged visitors from the bustle of the city and prepared them, as at Merion and as directed by the program, to enter the galleries with a sense of calm.

Williams's April 30 sketch floor plan showed this indirect entry sequence, now enriched by a contemplative pool that would extend into the building's generously sheltering entrance loggia. One would cross the pool on a causeway to reach the door. Because it had been determined that a mezzanine for educational programming could not be slipped into the gallery building, one of the garden courts had been replaced with two stacked classrooms serving the adjacent galleries.

From the start the architects had imagined that their building would be clad in limestone, like Cret's gallery in Merion. And, as there, a warm-hued stone was envisioned. A system of stone panels, to be attached by bronze clamps to the steel frame of the gallery wing and the poured-in-place concrete structure of the rest of the building, was being worked out by early May. Williams and Tsien explained to the board on May 16 that the varied sizes and syncopated pattern of the stone panels was inspired by the irregularities of African textiles, like the Kente cloth of Ghana. This also honored Barnes's incorporation of African motifs in the decoration of the original gallery.

While the "medallion" plan accommodated the program and addressed the parkway with dignity, the

TWENTIETH-CENTURY KENTE CLOTH. ASHANTI REGION, GHANA

large block containing the added services was straining the project's budget, and between the Building Committee meeting on June 19 and the board meeting on June 27, Williams determined that money could be saved and the central atrium could be opened with outside views if the western arm of the "C" was "eroded," converting it into an "L." This practical improvement in turn inspired an important artistic discovery: by sliding the L-shaped services building eastward, the entire length of the gallery facade could

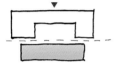

PLAN EVOLUTION.
JANUARY, JUNE,
SEPTEMBER 2008

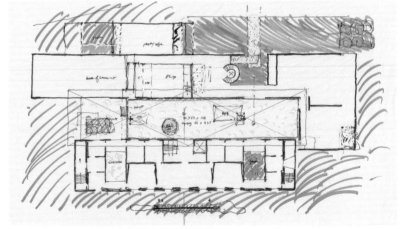

TOD WILLIAMS. SKETCH PLAN, AUGUST 7, 2008

be exposed to view in the atrium. Williams sketched this bold simplification on August 7. The water-crossing entrance would now be perfectly aligned with the garden inside the collection building, offering visitors an enticing glimpse of greenery from the door—as at the original site.

Williams and Tsien had emphasized in their writing and teaching that architecture should develop out of the plan—growing on the ground, as it were, in response to their evolving understanding of the site and the visitor's experience. Its massing—its three-dimensional form—should be the product of what was going on inside. True to this philosophy, it was only at this point that the architects decided that a great, roof-crowning monitor was the appropriate way to illuminate the central hall and thereby define the building's skyline. The monitor would not be a simple array of skylights, like the pleated roof that had previously been shown, but a giant box enclosing a heroic sculptural baffle that blocked direct light

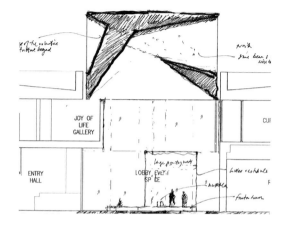

TOD WILLIAMS. SECTION OF "LIGHT CANYON," SEPTEMBER 3, 2008

(see page 49). They unveiled this topography of sun management, which they called a "light canyon," together with the marvelously simplified plan, to the Building Committee on September 5. The plan of the building, together with the assertive sculptural form that grew out of it to claim its place on the parkway, was now complete.

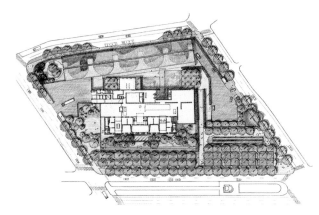

LAURIE OLIN. SITE PLAN, SEPTEMBER 4, 2008

Because of the mandate to integrate architecture and nature, the selection of a landscape architect was especially important, and after considering several prominent designers, Williams and Tsien's preference settled on Laurie Olin, whose Philadelphia-based, world-spanning firm had designed the gardens of the Getty Center in Los Angeles. Olin's work had been pre-viewed in August, but the September 5 meeting was its full debut. He lengthened the small water feature envisioned in the entrance garden into a long pool and reconfigured the system of waterways that Williams had shown at the doorway. Most striking graphically was the pattern of colorful plantings that he proposed for the green roof of what had been reduced to a surface parking lot. The contours of the design were inspired by the shape of the lunettes filled by Matisse's *The Dance* at Merion. The roof of the parking lot would eventually disappear to save money, but a green roof atop the administration block was kept in support of the quest for an ambitiously high energy-efficiency rating. During the fall, Olin simplified the system of pools in what came to be called the "contemplative garden" at the main door and replaced the long pool in the entrance garden at the corner of Twentieth Street with a water table planted with lilies.

A peek at the emergent design was offered to Mayor Michael Nutter on October 9 and to major supporters at

OPPOSITE: LAURIE OLIN. DESIGN FOR WATER TABLE, NOVEMBER 2008

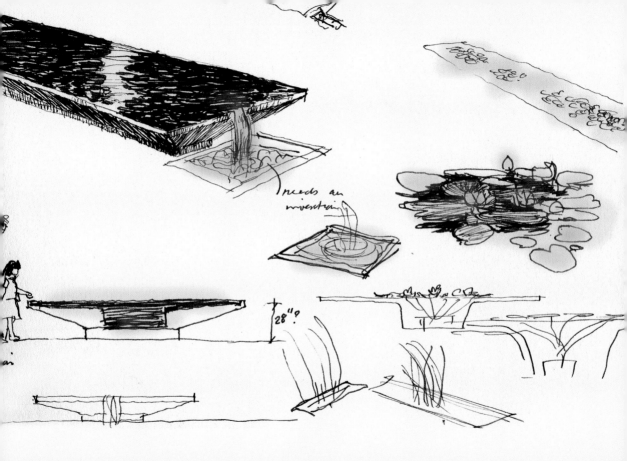

needs an
invertain

28"?

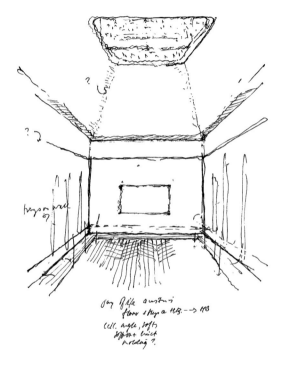

ABOVE: TOD WILLIAMS. SKETCH FOR *LE BONHEUR DE VIVRE*
ROOM, SEPTEMBER 16, 2009

a special event on October 15 at the Four Seasons Hotel.
The next morning the commencement of construction
was festively celebrated on the site, with the mayor
and Governor Edward Rendell in attendance.

Although the design was largely finalized, Williams
and Tsien were still struggling with a few details, most
notably how to display Matisse's *Le Bonheur de vivre* (also
called *The Joy of Life*), which in Merion was placed in the
stairway, with notorious disregard for viewers. The room
above the main entrance that had been designated as the
director's office at Merion would be available for other
uses in Philadelphia, and for nearly a year the architects
experimented with how to use it to display *Le Bonheur de
vivre,* toying with pushing it into the light court as a kind
of enclosed balcony. Finally rejecting that thinking in the
first set of colored presentation perspectives prepared
in early December, they showed the *Le Bonheur de vivre*
room only very slightly projecting behind a window.

OPPOSITE: PERSPECTIVE RENDERING OF THE LIGHT COURT, DECEMBER 2008
PREVIOUS SPREAD: RENDERING OF THE ENTRANCE GARDEN WITH WATER
TABLE, DECEMBER 2009

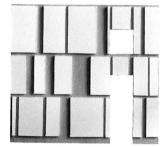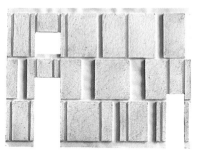

STUDY MODELS OF FACADE, SEPTEMBER 2008

During the first half of 2009 architects and client worked together on the important, character-defining details that would bring the building to life. The layout of the stone-paneling system had already been studied with drawings and models, determining how its horizontals would respect the window pattern of the Cret building while allowing the vertical joints to be composed asymmetrically. Stone samples were now examined, and in April four full-scale mock-ups of the wall system were erected on the site. On the basis of these, it was decided to pair two shades of tawny Israeli limestone, Ramon gray on the outside and Ramon gold in the interior light court. These were congenial, somewhat deferential companions of the brighter-hued Kasota dolomite of the Philadelphia Museum of Art.

The preliminary stone choice was refined by a visit to the quarries in the Negev desert in July (see page 2) and by the study of further mock-ups in August and November, during which three distinctive finishes were selected: a sandblasted and brushed patina finish for the exterior stone, a rough hand-chiseled surface for the light court, and a distinctive cuneiform pattern for smaller wall panels in the gallery garden. The mock-ups also allowed testing of the bronze and stone fins that the architects placed, in a syncopated rhythm, in some of the vertical reveals on the facade. These accents gave the new building some of the three-dimensionality of the classical cornices, window surrounds, and string courses at Merion.

Interior details received comparable attention. New, highly protective sun-screening glass would make it possible for modern visitors to see the garden through the full, uncurtained height of the floor-to-cornice windows. To maximize this effect, it was decided to give the new windows narrower muntins, a detail that was studied by comparing photographs of the existing conditions at Merion and digitally con-structed replacement alternatives. The window sashes were varnished rather than painted to unite them better with the woodwork (see page 44).

The oak trim of the galleries required even more sensitivity. There was no intention to replicate Cret's classical detailing, but neither was there a desire to do without moldings altogether—which Tsien said would be "like … you shaved off your eyebrows." For study purposes, the original woodwork profiles were copied in foam, and these were compared to simpler, squarer profiles, which aimed to have similar effects. Testing continued into 2010 with the construction of a full-size mock-up of one of the galleries, in which the Cret wood-work was faithfully reproduced in half the room and the other half installed with the plainer new designs. The architects' aim was to simplify and intensify the effects of the original moldings, applying a restraint that they judged to be both the heritage of a distinctive Pennsyl-vanian—perhaps Quaker—woodworking tradition and an expression of their own modernist sensibilities.

Lighting in the galleries was also studied seriously. Gillman was committed to showing the Barnes

collection under the best possible conditions, and to that end, the lighting consultants Fisher Marantz Stone were brought in shortly after Olin was appointed in 2008. After developing specifications for better artificial lighting, the designers turned their attention to natural light, and their analysis led to the momentous decision to light all the top-floor galleries from above. Only two of these rooms had been lit in that manner in Merion because of Cret and Barnes's preference for windows, all of which were retained in the parkway building. The stunningly beautiful top-lit galleries of the new Sainsbury Wing at the National Gallery in Britain offered persuasive evidence of what could be achieved, and under the direction of Paul Marantz (who had advised Venturi, Scott Brown and Associates in London), the design of a system of monitors to provide top lighting was investigated with the aid of miniature models and settled during the summer of 2009.

OPPOSITE: COMPARISON OF WINDOW SASH IN MAIN GALLERY, MERION, AND DIGITALLY RENDERED ALTERNATIVE FOR THE PARKWAY BUILDING, SPRING 2009

By the fall of 2009 the Barnes Foundation was ready to share the design. It was presented to the Philadelphia Art Commission, the city's design-review panel, on October 7, previewed for the press, and publicly unveiled at a morning event at Moore College of Art and Design on October 8.

Few of those who now saw the design for the first time had been privy to the complex, form-defining considerations that had powerfully pushed the architects to

FISHER MARANTZ STONE. LIGHTING STUDY MODEL OF ROOM 18, 2009

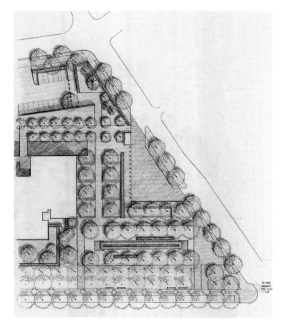

ABOVE: LAURIE OLIN. REVISED SITE PLAN, NOVEMBER 14, 2009
PREVIOUS SPREAD: THE BARNES FOUNDATION, SOUTHEAST FACADE

emphasize the Barnes's character as a quiet "gallery in a garden." They brought very different expectations to its evaluation—most importantly, that the new museum should be a lively presence on the Benjamin Franklin Parkway, long judged to be too thinly populated.

The images with which the design was presented did not help to bridge the gap in expectations. An aerial perspective emphasized the screen of trees between the building and the parkway and made the building seem quieter and more remote than it was. It clearly showed the large vehicular drop-off yard on Twentieth Street while hiding most of the carefully orchestrated pedestrian approach route. Equally but differently distorting was a low-vantage-point nighttime perspective from the west, which exaggerated both the scale and the lighting effects of the simple etched-glass box that was to enclose the "light canyon" over the central court (see page 49 for a similar daytime view). This made the design resemble just the kind of sculptural expressionism that its architects abjured.

The reviews in the *Philadelphia Inquirer* and the *New York Times* asked why the architects had not devised a livelier urban presence and why they had laid out such a circuitous route to the galleries. The Art Commission, while giving conceptual approval to the design, directed the architects to return with a reconsideration of both the pedestrian-access route and the Twentieth Street driveway.[19]

In retrospect, the architects and the clients acknowledged that these were useful suggestions, although any criticism of the controversial relocation project was cautiously received. By mid-November, they had reduced the size of the paved vehicle fore-court, and Olin had used the space to widen the path that led visitors away from the parkway and toward the entrance. There was room now to turn this walkway into a tree-lined allée (see pages 42–43). The Art Commission granted its final approval on January 6, 2010. Much of the work had already been put out to bid.

The building that opened its doors to visitors

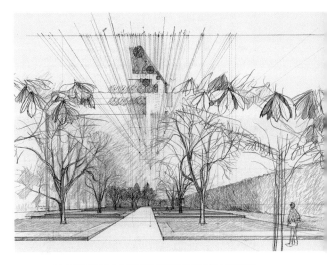

LAURIE OLIN. PERSPECTIVE OF REVISED ENTRANCE ALLÉE, LATE 2009

in spring 2012 possesses a simplicity that comes from the taming of a complex program, and it has a complex richness that derives from the marshaling of simple materials and methods. The pedestrian visitor

is ushered into the site along a graveled avenue, with a reflective water table at its center and a row of horse-chestnut trees on either side (see pages 62–63). Ahead, the building stands serenely, its simple geometry enriched by the textile-like pattern of warm-colored Ramon gray stone, each panel of which is composed of several pieces. The cutting of the Israeli limestone was done in Hebron on the West Bank, following drawings prepared by the architects, but with the actual stone pieces selected for their color by the stone-yard manager (see pages 70–71).

Turning to the right at the end of the water table, the museum visitor ascends a path framed by evergreen cedars. Ahead, a slender stainless steel sculpture by Ellsworth Kelly rises from the pavement. Made

RENDERING OF ENTRANCE CAUSEWAY AND ELLSWORTH KELLY'S *THE BARNES TOTEM*, DECEMBER 2011 possible through the generosity of the Neubauer Family Foundation, its abstracted tree-like profile mediates between the worlds of nature and the man made and marks a left turn into the allée of Japanese red maples that leads to the entrance (see page 50). This final approach route follows a still pool of water at the base of the building, turning at its end to cross to the doorway on a short causeway.

Quieted by this transition from the street side, the visitor now faces the recessed entrance, whose inner face is a wall of glass through which can be seen the bright atrium and, beyond it, the tree-filled garden court inside the Collection Gallery. A smaller pool lies straight ahead at the base of the glass, through which a carpet of mosaic, inspired by the liar's cloth pattern found in Kente textiles, can be seen on the floor (see pages 5 and 7). To the left, a Baule crocodile figure, like the pair that frames the door at Merion, is etched into a bronze panel. The actual door is to the right, inside which is the reception hall, from which one can directly enter the restaurant or descend by means of a large stair of walnut wood to the basement. There, a generous lobby, lit by the base of the gallery garden, gives access to the shop, auditorium, a large seminar room, and the library. From

RENDERING OF THE CAUSEWAY AND MAIN ENTRANCE, MAY 2010

the reception hall one may also rejoin the axis glimpsed from outside and proceed into the great light court, beyond which lie the collection galleries.

The light court offers views outward to the west, but it is filled with suffused sunshine that comes indirectly from above through the system of strongly sculpted baffles. These interior walls are of an even warmer shade of Israeli limestone, Ramon gold, and the surfaces are given depth by all-over hand chiseling (see page 4). While the lighting and views impart an outdoor feeling to this large space, its wooden floor and the comfortable furniture, designed by Williams and Tsien in collaboration with Knoll, give it an almost domestic sense as well. It is here that visitors wait for admission to the Collection Gallery.

The upper north wall of the light court is opened up by a continuous band of etched glass, behind which the work of the Foundation's staff goes on. The lower wall is paneled with acoustically absorbent boards, wrapped in felt that is composed of wool and silk. Designed and made by the Dutch textile artist Claudy Jongstra, who raises sheep and makes her own dyes, the strongly patterned panels add an animated, almost figural, element to the luminous interior.

The architects' support for modern craftsmen reverberates sympathetically across the years and miles with Albert Barnes's own proclivities, and this is apparent in the pair of great bronze gates designed for the entrance of the new Collection Gallery (see page 3). Inspired by African metalwork, their interwoven geometrical motifs frame the entrance. At Merion the comparable position was occupied by the tile work of Joe Allen, which was similarly informed by African art. Through both doorways, in Merion and in Philadelphia, the visitor is given a view of greenery, framed by the central window of the large main gallery, before plunging into the consuming experience of viewing the art collected by Albert Barnes as he wished it to be seen.

RENDERING OF "LIGHT CANYON," OCTOBER 2009

NOTES

[1] Unless otherwise noted, this and all other correspondence is in the Barnes Foundation Archives (BFA), organized by correspondents' names and dates.

[2] See Elizabeth Grossman, *The Civic Architecture of Paul Cret* (Cambridge: Cambridge University Press, 1996), pp. 112–115.

[3] This and the other quotations in this paragraph are from Cret, "The Building for the Barnes Foundation," *The Arts,* vol. 3 (Jan. 1923), p. 8.

[4] Barnes to Cret, Nov. 22, 1922, BFA.

[5] Usefully summarized in Mary Ann Meyers, *Albert Barnes and the Science of Philanthropy: Art, Education, and African-American Culture,* revised edition (New Brunswick, NJ, and London: Transaction Publishers, 2009), pp. 72–73.

[6] Cret's unsent correspondence is in the Cret papers, collection 295, Rare Book & Manuscript Library Collections, University of Pennsylvania (CPUP).

[7] Cret to Barnes [Sep. 28, 1928], BFA. A dated, typed copy is in CPUP, folder 30.

[8] Cret to Barnes [Feb. 26, 1924] (unsent), CPUP, folder 30.

[9] William J. Conlen to Cret, Oct. 28, 1924, CPUP, folder 85.

[10] Barnes to Cret, Nov. 11, 1924, BFA.

[11] The final accounts are in the Cret papers, Athenaeum of Philadelphia, box 3, #27.F.132, 1 of 3.

[12] Cret, "The Buildings of the Barnes Foundation in Merion, Pa.," *Architecture,* vol. 53, no. 1 (Jan. 1926), p. 2.

[13] This and subsequent quotations are from Polshek Partnership Architects, "The Barnes Foundation: Programming & Site Analysis," Jan. 2, 2007, BFA.

[14] "The Barnes Foundation Petitions Court to Move Gallery into Philadelphia," press release, Sept. 24, 2002, BFA.

15 Williams and Tsien, interview with author, July 21, 2011.

16 Williams and Tsien, "New Philadelphia Facility: The Barnes Foundation, Merion, Pennsylvania" [n.d., c. Apr. 1, 2007], BFA.

17 Williams, interview with author, July 21, 2011. All meetings of the board and Building Committee are documented in the PowerPoint presentations, collection of TWBTA.

18 Williams and Tsien, "Slowness," *2G International Architecture Review,* vol. 26, no. 9 (1999), pp. 130–143.

19 Nicolai Ouroussoff, "Architects Reimagine the Barnes Collection," *New York Times,* Oct. 7, 2009, http://www.nytimes.com/2009/10/07/arts/design/07barnes.html (accessed Aug. 13, 2011); Inga Saffron, "Changing Skyline: Perking up the Parkway," *Philadelphia Inquirer,* Oct. 16, 2009, http://www.philly.com/philly/home/20091016_Changing_Skyline_Perking_up_the_Parkway.html (accessed Aug. 13, 2011).

A SECTION OF THE FRIEZE IN THE MAIN ROOM, BARNES FOUNDATION, PHILADELPHIA

First published in the United States of America in 2012 by

Skira Rizzoli Publications, Inc.
300 Park Avenue South
New York, NY 10010
www.rizzoliusa.com

in association with

The Barnes Foundation
2025 Benjamin Franklin Parkway
Philadelphia, PA 19103
www.barnesfoundation.org

Library of Congress Control Number: 2012934728
ISBN: 978-0-8478-3892-9 (Skira Rizzoli)
ISBN: 978-0-9848-5781-4 (Barnes Foundation)

Copyright © 2012 by The Barnes Foundation

Editor: Philip Reeser
Design: Skelton Design
Production: Kaija Markoe

Printed and bound in the United States

2012 2013 2014 2015 2016 / 10 9 8 7 6 5 4 3 2 1

IMAGE CREDITS:
Barnes Foundation Archives: pp. 10, 16–17, 18, 26, 39
Brooklyn Digital Foundry: pp. 42–43, 49, 50, 62–63, 74, 77
Giles Ashford: p. 68 (source photograph)
Fairmount Park Historic Resource Archive,
   Philadelphia Parks & Recreation: p. 15
Fisher Marantz Stone: p. 69
Michael Moran/OTTO: endpapers, frontispiece, pp. 4, 7, 12, 45, 70–71, 79
Newark Museum/Art Resource, NY: p. 57
OLIN: pp. 46, 60, 61, 72, 73
Paul P. Cret Collection, Athenaeum of Philadelphia: pp. 1, 21, 23, 28, 33
Paul Philippe Cret Collection, The Architectural Archives, University of
   Pennsylvania: pp. 19 (right), 24
Rare Book and Manuscript Library, University of Pennsylvania: pp. 8, 22
Rick Echelmeyer: cover (hinge), pp. 11, 16–17, 25, 30, 34, 35, 40, 41
Robert Coldwell Photography: p. 20
Tod Williams Billie Tsien Architects: cover (sketch), pp. 2, 3, 5, 9, 10, 44,
   51, 52, 53, 54, 55, 56, 58, 59, 64, 65, 66, 68 (modification of Ashford
   photograph), 75
Urban Archives, Temple University Libraries/Associated Press: p. 19 (left)

COVER IMAGES:
Hinge. Iron, 8 ½ x 5 ½ x ½ in. The Barnes Foundation, Philadelphia. 01.13.67
Tod Williams. Sketch for entrance gates to Collection Gallery on the Benjamin
Franklin Parkway, Philadelphia, c. August 2011